Twenty Little Log Cabin Quilts

With Full-Size Templates

Gwen Marston

Illustrated by Pat Holly

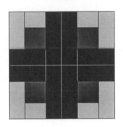

Dover Publications, Inc.
New York

Acknowledgments

All quilts designed and made by Gwen Marston.

All illustrations by Pat Holly

Thanks to Laura Bos for proofreading

Photographs by The Keva Partnership

This book is dedicated to all of the women who have attended the annual Beaver Island Quilt Retreat.

Other Books by the Author

With the exception of *Q is for Quilt, Twenty Little Amish Quilts* and *Twenty Little Pinwheel Quilts,* all books are co-authored by Joe Cunningham.

American Beauties: Rose and Tulip Quilts. American Quilter's Society, Paducah, Kentucky, 1988.

Amish Quilting Patterns. Dover Publications, Inc., New York, 1987.

Mary Schafer and Her Quilts. Michigan State University Press, East Lansing, Michigan, 1990.

Q is for Quilt. Michigan State University Press, 1987.

Quilting with Style: Principles for Great Pattern Design. American Quilter's Society, 1993.

Sets and Borders. American Quilter's Society, 1987.

70 Classic Quilting Patterns. Dover Publications, Inc., 1987

Twenty Little Amish Quilts. Dover Publications, Inc., 1993.

Twenty Little Patchwork Quilts. Dover Publications, Inc., 1990.

Twenty Little Pinwheel Quilts. Dover Publications, Inc., 1994.

Published in Canada by General Publishing Company, Ltd., 30 Lesmill Road, Don Mills, Toronto, Ontario.

Published in the United Kingdom by Constable and Company, Ltd., 3 The Lanchesters, 162–164 Fulham Palace Road, London W6 9ER.

Bibliographical Note

Twenty Little Log Cabin Quilts: With Full-Size Templates is a new work, first published by Dover Publications, Inc., in 1995.

Library of Congress Cataloging-in-Publication Data

Marston, Gwen.
      Twenty little log cabin quilts : with full-size templates / Gwen Marston ; illustrated by Pat Holly.
            p.   cm. — (Dover needlework series)
      ISBN 0-486-28809-9 (pbk.)
      1. Patchwork—Patterns.   2. Log cabin quilts.   3. Miniature quilts.   I. Title.   II. Series.
TT835.M37825 1995
746.46'0228—dc20   95-17401
                                                                                              CIP

Manufactured in the United States of America
Dover Publications, Inc., 31 East 2nd Street, Mineola, N.Y. 11501

GENERAL INSTRUCTIONS

The basic Log Cabin block begins in the center with a square and is made up of strips of fabric called "logs." These logs are sewn on one at a time until all four sides of the center square are covered (*Figure 1*). More logs are added (*Figure 2*), then more, around and around (*Figure 3*), until the block is the desired size. Traditionally, the center square is red to symbolize the warmth of a fireplace.

Figure 1

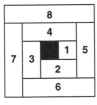

Figure 2

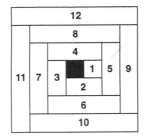

Figure 3

The traditional Log Cabin block is simple, but set a number of blocks together and the fun begins. Since the mid-1800s, generation after generation has experimented with Log Cabin sets. Many of these traditional sets have intriguing names like "Barn Raising," "Streak of Lightning" and "Straight Furrows" (*Figures 4, 5 and 6*). By computer calculation, over 1000 set variations of Log Cabin have been recorded, and the experimentation is far from finished.

In addition, the basic block can be distorted to give different effects. Making logs on one side of the block wider than the logs on the other side can produce a circular swirl when a large number of blocks are set together. Increasing or decreasing the width of the logs as they are added creates another effect.

All of this Log Cabin experimentation requires risk. Fabric is expensive and time is precious. One solution is to make small quilts. Multiple small experiments can be tried in less time than is required by one full-size quilt. Fabric purchase is minimal—often leftovers from past projects can be used effectively to help create new small quilts. Not much time and not much money is invested in a small quilt, so risk is cut to an acceptable level.

In general, Log Cabin blocks are easy to construct. They do not present the quilter with complex points to match, curves to struggle with or a maze of pattern pieces to fit together. Each of the 20 quilts in this book does, however, present its own unique challenge. Consequently, I have arranged the quilt patterns in order from least to most difficult to construct, as follows:

Fabric

All of the quilts in this book were made of 100% cotton fabric. Color and print choices offer a major opportunity to individualize your quilt. If you wish to closely copy any of my 20 quilts, you have my blessing. I know my own study of and borrowing from nineteenth-century quilts has shaped what I do today.

The traditional Log Cabin block is made with light fabrics on one side and dark fabrics on the other (*Figure 7*). When the lights and darks of multiple blocks are organized, they produce an overall graphic pattern. High contrast in the colors you choose creates a dramatic quilt; low contrast in colors creates a softer, more subtle effect.

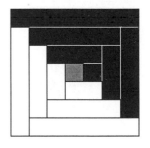

Figure 7

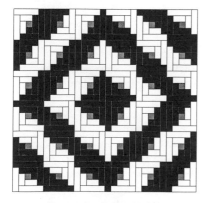

Figure 4—Barn Raising

Figure 5—Streak of Lightning

Figure 6—Straight Furrows

Some of my 20 quilts were made in two colors; others use scraps of a large variety of light and dark colors. Some were made with all solids, others with all prints and still others with a combination of both.

Remember, small quilts need only small amounts of fabric. Leftovers and large scraps will suffice. If purchasing fabric, ¼-yard pieces are more than adequate for any of the quilt tops, with a ½- to ¾-yard piece of fabric for the backing.

I recommend washing all quilt fabric for the following reasons:

- To reduce shrinkage later. Most modern 100% cotton has little shrinkage, but a quick wash now can prevent problems later.
- To test for color fastness. Repeat the final rinse until the water runs clear. If still in doubt, place the fabric, while still wet, on a piece of scrap muslin or a white paper towel to see if the color runs. If it runs, select another fabric and dispose of the offender.
- To remove manufacturer's sizing. Removal of sizing makes your project easier to hand-quilt.

Since small quilts require only small amounts of fabric, hand washing is convenient, and has the added advantage of allowing you to see the rinse water without having to catch the washing machine at just the right moment of its cycle. With hand washing, color fastness is more easily judged and tested.

Press all newly washed fabric to increase cutting accuracy and ease. Cut off the selvedges after pressing.

Cutting Logs and Center Squares

Rotary Cutting Method

The easiest, fastest and most accurate way to cut strips of fabric is to use a rotary cutter and cutting mat. Here is a list of ten rotary cutting principles to keep in mind.

1. Use your cutter carefully. It is very sharp.
2. Make sure you close the blade every time you lay the cutter down.
3. Change the blade as soon as it begins to dull.
4. If you are right-handed, place the fabric on the cutting mat so that it extends to the right.
5. Use a ruler and cutting mat that have both vertical and horizontal grids.
6. Always cut away from yourself.
7. Hold the ruler firmly with your left hand.
8. Trim off the uneven edge of the fabric, making it square to the selvedge edge.
9. Position the ruler to the proper width and cut the fabric with one, clean stroke.
10. Squaring your fabric first produces a cut more accurately on the grain. Cutting strips on the grain reduces stretching and distortion of the blocks later.

With the selvedge edges together, fold your fabric in half lengthwise and press. Fold it lengthwise again, so it is in four layers. At this point, a quick second press with your iron will help the fabric layers stick together and help prevent the shifting that causes inaccuracy. Position the ruler at the width called for and cut an appropriate number of strips. Start with two or three strips per fabric—more can

be cut as needed. Repeat the process for each of the fabrics to be used in the Log Cabin blocks.

Leave the strips folded in fourths, so you can later cut four logs or center squares at a time.

The individual instructions give you the lengths and the number of logs and center squares you need to cut from each fabric. With your rotary cutter, cut four at a time from your strips. Organize the logs by color and length on the left side of your sewing machine, so you can find them easily during block construction.

Scissors Method

The logs can, of course, be cut with scissors. All the templates needed to make these quilts are printed on lightweight cardboard in the center of the book. If a template is to be used many times, you may wish to make it even more durable by gluing it to a second sheet of lightweight cardboard or tracing it onto transparent plastic.

All templates include the seam allowance and are the exact size needed to cut logs and center squares for machine piecing. I find I can accurately cut up to four layers of fabric at a time. This is a timesaver, since only the top layer needs the cutting line marked. Make sure the layers are pressed flat. Ironing helps hold the layers together and prevent shifting.

Carefully lay all templates on the straight grain of the fabric. The major problem with Log Cabin block construction is distortion caused by logs stretching out of shape. Paying particular attention to the straight grain of the fabric now will help prevent problems with stretching later.

Draw around the template with a regular lead pencil or a white or silver Berol Verithin pencil (available at art or drafting supply shops, as well as many quilt and fabric stores).

Accurate cutting is especially important for machine sewing, as you will be following the edge of the cut fabric to guide your sewing line.

Thread

Log Cabin blocks are often half dark and half light in color, making selection of a thread color a problem. Changing thread with the addition of each log would be ridiculously time-consuming. Depending on the overall tone of the quilt, I used either all white or all black thread for each of these quilts. I always sew with 100% cotton thread, but this is simply one person's preference.

Block Construction

A number of methods of Log Cabin block construction have been invented over the years. Three often-used methods are:

- using a muslin or paper foundation
- sewing onto a long piece of fabric
- precutting strips plus chain piecing

Sewing on a muslin or paper foundation is very accurate, but very time-consuming. Sewing onto a long piece of fabric is fast, but lacks accuracy due to the stretching that can occur when sewing the block to the long strip.

I recommend precutting the logs. This way, you know

each log is exactly the right length. This helps prevent stretching a log and distorting the block.

Chain piecing is the second half of the method I recommend. Chain piecing as a block construction method saves time and helps keep the work organized. Instead of making one block at a time, you construct all the blocks in an assembly-line fashion. Sew all the number one logs to all their center squares, one after another, without cutting the thread between them. Then clip the threads between the blocks and begin the process over again by sewing the number two logs to the center squares. Continue the process, being careful to always add the logs in a consistent, clockwise way.

Sewing a consistent seam allowance is particularly important when making small quilts. Even slight discrepancies cause problems. I recommend that you build up a layer of tape on the plate of your sewing machine exactly ¼″ away from the needle. You can use masking tape, electrical tape or moleskin (available in most drugstores; sold to comfort tender spots on feet, it is about ⅛″ thick and has a sticky backing which will adhere nicely to your sewing machine plate). The idea is to make a ridge to guide the edge of your fabric consistently ¼″ away from the needle.

As you sew, make sure the seams are all lying toward the outside of the block. A light finger-pressing will do the job. This way, your finished blocks will lie square and flat. This makes joining the blocks together later easier, and helps ensure a quilt top which will also lie flat.

Standard Log Cabin blocks are constructed by adding the logs around and around. However, variations of the standard block demand variations in block construction. My quilts that include Courthouse Steps blocks and Cornerstones have detailed block construction directions.

Pressing

Pressing the seams with an iron is not necessary, or even advisable, until all the blocks are completed. It is easy to stretch a block out of square by pressing it during the construction process. I have found that I have better results by not pressing until all the blocks are completed.

All the seams should be pressed toward the outside edges of the blocks.

Because there are so many seams, care must be taken not to distort the blocks as they are being pressed. First, press each block lightly on the top side. Check the back of the block to make sure the seams are all lying toward the outside edges. If not, lightly press the back of the block, first encouraging the seams to lie in the correct direction. Next, use a steam iron, or mist or "spritz" the top side of the block using a recycled spray bottle or plant mister and press the block again thoroughly.

Sewing the Blocks Together

Now that all the blocks are sewn and pressed, it is time to lay them out in rows. Follow the quilt diagram if you wish, or experiment with your own ideas of block placement.

The blocks will now be sewn together into horizontal rows. Then the rows will be joined to complete the quilt top (*Figure 8*).

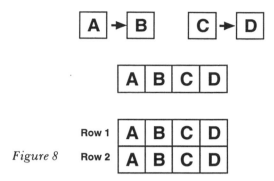

Figure 8

I have a system for chain piecing the blocks and rows together. This system keeps me from accidentally flipping a block or row of blocks the wrong way. In addition, chain piecing is faster and eliminates the need to trim threads at the beginning and end of each seam.

Place a pin at the left side of block A in every row, as a reminder that this is the first block in a row. Sew block A and block B of row 1 together. Without clipping the thread, sew block A and block B of row 2 together.

Leaving the second set of blocks attached to the machine, clip the thread between the first and second set of sewn blocks. Lay out the first set in its original position on your table. Pick up block C of row 1 and sew it to the first set. The pin you placed at the left side of block A now prevents you from making the mistake of sewing block C to the wrong end of the first row.

Clip the thread between the two sets of sewn blocks now attached to your machine and lay row 2 in its original position. Pick up the row 2 block C and sew it on. Continue in this way until all the blocks are joined into rows, then remove all your reminder pins.

Place a new reminder pin at the top of block A in row 1 and block A in row 3. Sew row 1 and row 2 together. Then sew row 3 and row 4 together. The pins are located in the beginning of the odd-numbered rows 1, 3, 5. Remember to never sew two pinned rows together, and you can't go wrong. Continue sewing the rows together until the top is completed and ready for pressing.

Press the top, making sure all these new seams joining blocks and rows lie toward the outside edges of the quilt. The top should lie flat to ensure an accurate measurement for the borders.

Borders

Not all of these quilts have borders. For some, it is the binding that frames the quilt. This is always an option, as is the addition of multiple borders. The important consideration is that the border must always complement the quilt. It should never overpower or distract from the quilt's impact.

If you decide to add a border, measure your quilt top carefully, so you can cut borders in exact lengths. If you just sew on a length of fabric and then trim it, the borders are more likely to pucker or ripple. It is just too easy to stretch the body of the quilt or the border strip.

Measure for the two longer sides first. Measure across the middle of the quilt top to obtain the most accurate measurement. Cut the two borders. Pin the borders onto the quilt top, beginning with the ends. Pin the midpoint, then pin about every 4″ or 5″. Sew these side borders and press the seam allowance toward the outside edges. With the side borders joined to the quilt top, now measure the midpoint for the top and bottom borders. Repeat the above process, cutting the two border strips, pinning for accuracy before sewing, then sewing and pressing.

Backing

Give the backing fabric some thought so it adds something to your quilt. I chose interesting prints for the backing of many of these little quilts. Others have solid color backings. Sometimes I chose fabrics that appeared in the quilt top for a unifying echo effect. Other times, I chose a fabric which was a surprise, something completely unexpected and fun.

Cut the backing so that it measures at least 1½″ larger than the quilt top all the way around. In other words, cut the backing at least 3″ longer and 3″ wider than the quilt.

Batting

The most important consideration when selecting a batting for these small quilts is the thickness. Thick batts look too heavy and bulky in small quilts, so choose a thin batt.

I used both cotton and polyester batts in these quilts. Polyester batting is easier to quilt through and requires less quilting than a cotton batt; still, I like the look and feel of natural cotton batting. I used cotton when the quilt top was made of dark solid colors. Polyester batting sometimes "beards"; that is, some of the fibers work through to the surface of the fabric. This doesn't happen with cotton batting.

Cut the batting slightly smaller than the quilt back.

Quilting and Tying

These quilts can be hand- or machine-quilted. The quilts that are made with ½″-wide finished logs are not quilted. The many seams would make quilting very difficult. These quilts are tied, some on the back and some on the top. If you lap quilt, use a hoop or tie the quilt, you will need to baste the three layers together.

For both quilting and basting, I think I get the best results from stretching the quilt in a full-size frame that I make myself. It is simply four 1″ × 2″ pine boards about 36″ long. To each board, I staple a length of sturdy fabric that sticks out about ½″ over the long edge of the board. Baste the edges of the quilt backing to two of the boards, lay these across the other two boards and secure them with small C-clamps. Pin the two loose edges of the quilt back to the fabric strips every 1″ to 2″. Spread the batting over the backing and smooth it out. Lay the quilt top on the batting and pin around the edges through all layers. Check to make sure it is stretched tightly and that there are no wrinkles in the backing or the top.

Hand Quilting

The quilting stitch is a small running stitch that holds all three layers of the quilt together. It is done with a single strand of cotton thread and a short needle called a "between." The larger the number of the needle, the smaller the needle. I use a number 9 between for all of my quilting. Experiment with size until you find the needle comfortable for you. I suggest you try to find one with a large eye for ease in threading. You can buy special quilting thread that is treated with a coating that makes it easy to thread on the needle.

The needle is guided through the layers of the quilt with a thimble on the middle finger of the right hand. The left hand is underneath the quilt and feels the needle as it goes through the layers of the quilt. The quilting stitch is done in a rocking motion, up and down, building 4 to 6 stitches on the needle before it is pulled through. Describing this technique is much more complicated than the actual quilting process. The best way to learn to quilt is to see it done. Find someone who can sit with you and show you how to hand-quilt.

Because the logs in some of these quilts are very narrow, I chose to hand-quilt them through the center of the log. Several of the quilts with large center squares are quilted in an "X" through each center square.

Machine Quilting

Some of these quilts are machine quilted, which is, of course, much faster than hand quilting. I used regular 100% cotton thread in a color that blended with the predominant tone of the quilt top. If the backing was a different color, I used a thread color in the bobbin that blended with the backing. Set the stitch size at about 15 stitches per inch. Select a quilting pattern with as few starts and stops as possible to make your quilting more efficient.

Tying

Many antique log cabin quilts were tied, some on the top and some on the back. The choice depends on whether you wish the ties to show up as part of the overall design, or wish to play them down by making them less visible on the top.

The most frequently used placement of ties is in the corners and centers of the blocks. Embroidery floss, pearl cotton, yarn and crochet threads are all viable choices for tying material. You will need a long needle with a large eye, such as a darning needle.

Tying is done with a simple square knot made by tying right over left and under, then left over right and under (*Figure 9*).

Figure 9

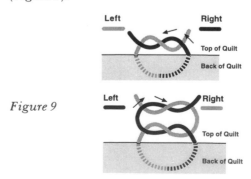

Work on a flat surface that won't be hurt if you scratch it with the needle. I used my large rotary cutting mat as a tying surface. To help keep the quilt layers from shifting, pin about every 4″ around all four edges, keeping the pins perpendicular to the edges of the quilt. Tie with the quilt flat on the surface. From the top, stick the needle down through all the layers (quilt top, batting and backing), turn the needle and pull it up to the surface making a small stitch approximately ⅛″ long. Now tie a square knot and clip the thread. I usually clip my threads about ½″ to ¾″ long.

Binding

Adding the binding to Log Cabin quilts poses a problem because the edges are often quite open. I stabilize the edges of the quilt before adding the binding. First pin the edges of the quilt together, then machine stay-stitch or hand-baste all the way around the quilt. Sew about ⅛″ from the edge to guarantee that the binding will cover the basting.

All of the quilts were finished with a separate, single, continuous binding cut on the straight of the fabric.

To make single binding on the straight, follow the same procedure as rotary cutting strips to make logs. Fold the fabric into four layers, square the end of the fabric and cut 1¼″-wide strips. Two strips of 45″ fabric will make enough binding for these small quilts.

Sew the two strips together and finger-press the seam open. This is the only time I press seams open—it distributes the seam allowance evenly, making the binding lie flatter.

Begin adding the binding in the middle [...] quilt top. Never begin binding at a corne[...] make turning that corner almost impos[...] binding along the edge of the quilt top with[...] together. Start sewing on the binding, leavin[...] the binding loose. Sew a consistent ¼″ seam.

Mitering the corners is easy once you get the hang of it. Sew your seam to exactly ¼″ from the bottom edge of the quilt. Lift the presser foot and pull the quilt away from the sewing machine. Fold the binding up and away from the quilt at a 45° angle (*Figure 10*). Now fold the binding back down (*Figure 11*). Carefully place the needle ¼″ in from both sides of the corner, line up the binding with the outer edge of the quilt and continue sewing across the bottom of the quilt.

Continue around in this manner, stopping about 4″ away from your first stitches. Remove the quilt completely from the sewing machine and lay it on a flat surface.

Now, join the two ends. Lay both ends along the edge of the quilt, overlapping each other (*Figure 12*). Draw a pencil line along the edge of the binding that is lying on top. Add ½″ and cut off the extra binding. Join the ends with a ¼″ seam allowance and finger-press the seam open (*Figure 13*). Finish stitching the binding in place.

Once the binding is sewn on, lay the quilt right side up on your cutting mat. Lay a quilter's ruler along the edge of the quilt and trim backing and batting exactly ¼″ beyond the seam. Fold the binding over the back of the quilt; roll the seam allowance under and blindstitch it in place.

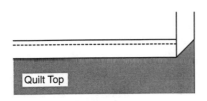

Figure 10

Figure 12

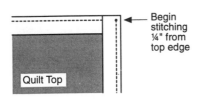

Figure 11

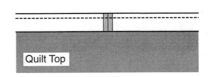

Figure 13

Plaid Log Cabin

Shown on inside front cover

16" x 20"
4" blocks - 20 blocks set 4 x 5

Templates needed: A, B, C, D

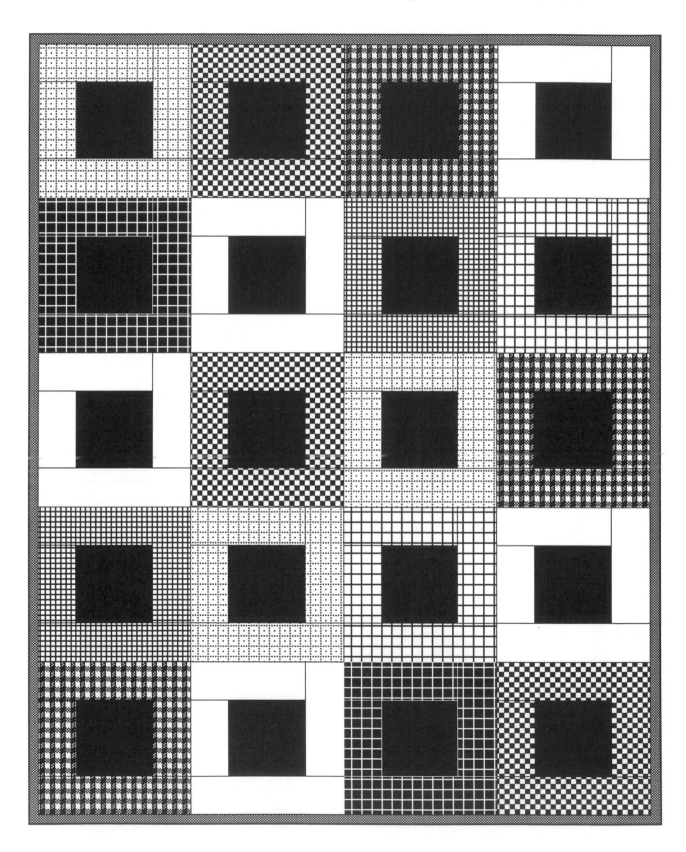

Plaid Log Cabin

This is a simple log cabin variation: the center square is large, and just one set of logs is added to frame the center. The blocks finish 4". The center square is 2" finished, and the logs are 1" finished. Center squares are a brown print, and the logs are plaids.

Cutting Instructions:

When selecting fabrics for this quilt, a variety of plaids was used in the different blocks for the logs. Then for each block, the same plaid was used for all four logs. All twenty center squares were cut from the same print.

Following the general directions, cut pieces either using templates and scissors or rotary cutter

	Per Block		Total
A	1 center		20 center
B	1	cut from	20
C	2	same fabric	40
D	1		20

Center Square

A
2½" x 2½"

Logs

B
1½" x 2½"

D
1½" x 4½"

C
1½" x 3½"

To Assemble:

Blocks:

Refer to general instructions for how to sew pieces together into blocks.

Start with center square A and add log B.
Next, add log C, another log C, then finish the block by sewing on log D.

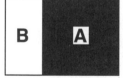

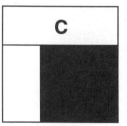

Rows:

Refer to the section in the general instructions called "Sewing the Blocks Together". This explains construction of rows into a finished top.

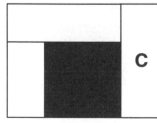

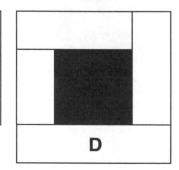

Barn Raising
Shown on inside front cover

15¾" x 18"
2¼" blocks - 56 blocks set 7 x 8

Templates needed: E, F, G

Barn Raising

Barn Raising is my favorite log cabin set. The first quilt I ever made used this set.

This quilt is asymmetrical. Only a square quilt will be symmetrical when using Barn Raising for the set. The fabrics are mostly solid colors with the addition of just a few prints, making these prints happy surprises.

Barn raising needs many blocks to show the pattern effectively. To accomplish this, I used a simplified block going around the center square only once, with two light logs followed by two dark logs. Strong contrast between the light and dark colors helps the pattern emerge.

This quilt is machine quilted in the ditch with black thread.

Cutting Instructions:

When selecting fabrics for the logs, a variety of different solids, light and dark, was used, plus a few prints. The center squares were all cut from the same red fabric.

Following the general directions, cut pieces either using templates and scissors or rotary cutter

	Per Block	Total
E	1 center, 1 light	56 center, 56 light
F	1 light, 1 dark	56 light, 56 dark
G	1 dark	56 dark

Center Square

E
1¼" x 1¼"

Logs

E
1¼" x 1¼"

G
1¼" x 2¾"

F
1¼" x 2"

To Assemble:

Blocks:

Refer to general instructions for how to sew pieces together into blocks.

Start with center square E and add light log E.
Next, add light log F, dark log F, then finish the block by sewing on dark log G.

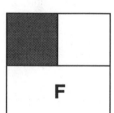

Rows:

Refer to the section in the general instructions called "Sewing the Blocks Together". This explains construction of rows into a finished top. Following the color photograph and drawing, arrange the blocks in rows to achieve the barn raising set.

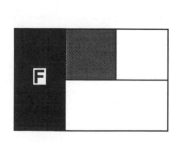
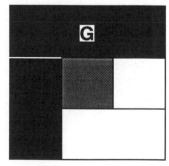

Straight Furrows

Shown on inside front cover

15" x 18¾"
3¾" blocks - 20 blocks set 4 x 5

Templates needed: E, F, G, H, I

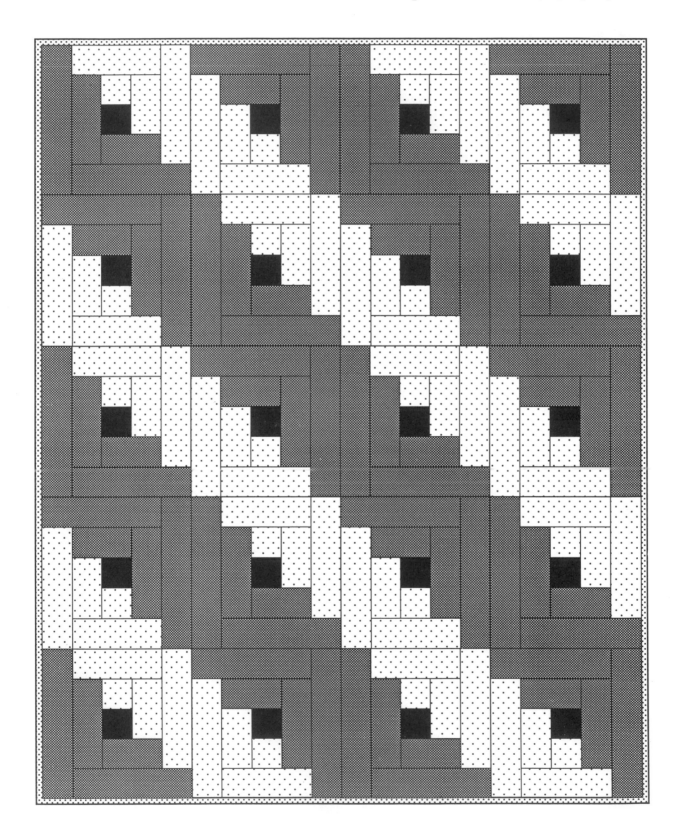

Straight Furrows

Pat Holly sent me this beautiful peachy floral print, and I couldn't wait to use it. The straight furrows pattern reads clearly in this quilt, even though all the colors are soft. You can get a strong effect by using one busy print and a mixture of solids. Hand quilted.

Cutting Instructions:

For this quilt, the center squares were all cut from the same dark fabric. The "dark" side of the block was cut from the same floral print. The "light" side was cut from a variety of light solid fabrics.

Following the general directions, cut pieces either using templates and scissors or rotary cutter

	Per Block	Total
E	1 center, 1 light	20 center, 20 light
F	1 light, 1 dark	20 light, 20 dark
G	1 light, 1 dark	20 light, 20 dark
H	1 light, 1 dark	20 light, 20 dark
I	1 dark	20 dark

Center Square

E
1¼" x 1¼"

Logs

E
1¼" x 1¼"

F
1¼" x 2"

G
1¼" x 2¾"

H
1¼" x 3½"

I
1¼" x 4¼"

To Assemble:

Blocks:

Refer to general instructions for how to sew pieces together into blocks.

Start with center square E and add log E.
Next, add light log F, then dark log F. Continue adding logs G, H, and I.

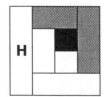

Rows:

Refer to the section in the general instructions called "Sewing the Blocks Together". This explains construction of rows into a finished top. Following the color photograph and drawing, be sure to arrange the blocks so the colors form the straight furrows pattern.

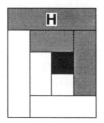
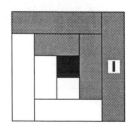

13

Zig Zag

Shown on inside front cover

15" x 18¾"
3¾" blocks - 20 blocks set 4 x 5

Templates needed: E, F, G, H, I

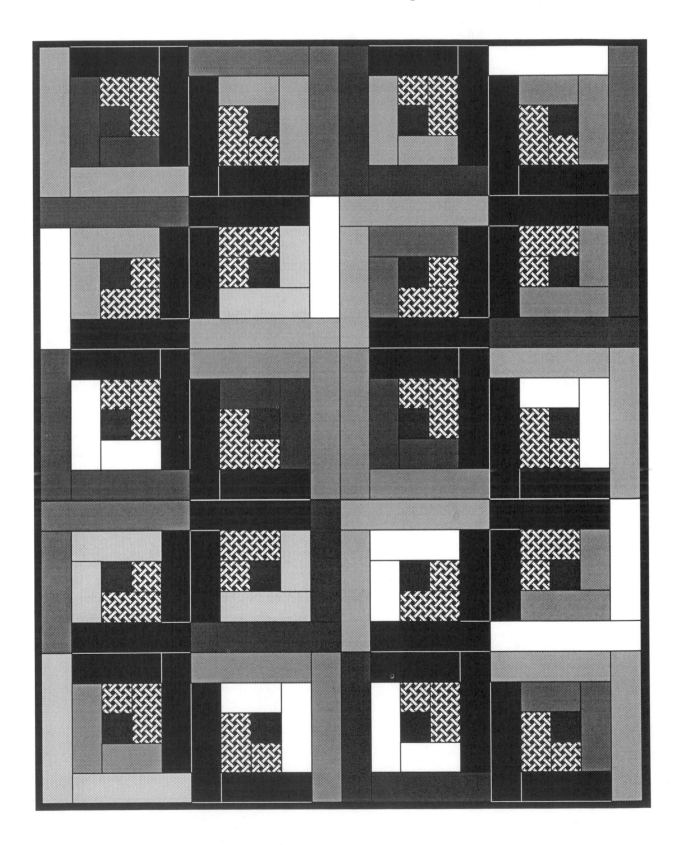

Zig Zag

This quilt is composed of bright colors and one strong print, which is always in the same position. The bright colored logs are a variety of solids. The quilt is hand quilted in white thread.

Cutting Instructions:

For this quilt, the center squares were all cut from the same red fabric. The "dark" side of the block was cut from two fabrics. The longer logs were cut from black fabric, and the shorter logs were cut from a bold print. The "light" side was cut from a variety of bright, solid fabrics.

Following the general directions, cut pieces either using templates and scissors or rotary cutter.

	Per Block	Total
E	1 center, 1 bold	20 center, 20 bold
F	1 light, 1 bold	20 light, 20 bold
G	1 light, 1 dark	20 light, 20 dark
H	1 light, 1 dark	20 light, 20 dark
I	1 light	20 light

Center Square

E
1¼" x 1¼"

Logs

E
1¼" x 1¼"

F
1¼" x 2"

G
1¼" x 2¾"

H
1¼" x 3½"

I
1¼" x 4¼"

To Assemble:

Blocks:

Refer to general instructions for how to sew pieces together into blocks.

Start with center square E and add bold log E.
Next, add bold log F, then light log F. Continue adding logs G, H, and I.

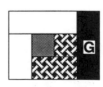

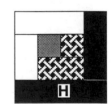

Rows:

Refer to the section in the general instructions called "Sewing the Blocks Together". This explains construction of rows into a finished top. Be sure to arrange the blocks carefully to maintain the zig zag pattern.

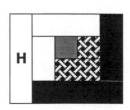

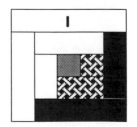

On Point

Shown on inside back cover

17¼" x 19¼"
3¾" blocks - 13 blocks set on point

Templates needed: E, F, G, H, I, J, K

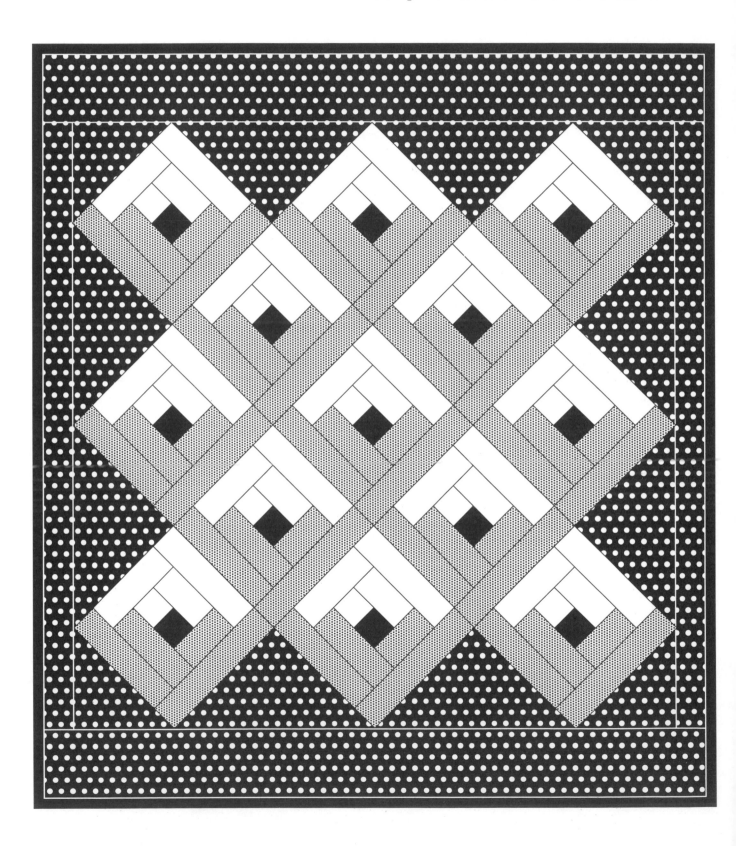

On Point

In this quilt, thirteen solid color blocks are set on point and surrounded with black-and-white polka-dots. One print was used in the bottom center block to add unexpected charm. The backing fabric is a paisley Alexander Hamilton print given to me by Carol Zimmerman. This quilt is machine quilted in black thread on the top and turquoise thread on the back. By using thread which echoes the predominant color of the fabric, the machine-quilting lines blend in well.

Cutting Instructions:

For this quilt, the center squares were (almost) all cut from the same red fabric. The "dark" and "light" sides of the block were cut from a variety of solid fabrics.

Following the general directions, cut pieces either using templates and scissors or rotary cutter

	Per Block	Total
E	1 center, 1 light	13 center, 13 light
F	1 light, 1 dark	13 light, 13 dark
G	1 light, 1 dark	13 light, 13 dark
H	1 light, 1 dark	13 light, 13 dark
I	1 dark	13 dark
J		8 polka-dot
K		4 polka-dot

Side Borders: Cut 1¼" x length of top

Top & Bottom Borders:
Cut 2¼" x length of top after adding side borders. See general directions.

Center Square

E
1¼" x 1¼"

Logs

E
1¼" x 1¼"

F
1¼" x 2"

G
1¼" x 2¾"

H
1¼" x 3½"

I
1¼" x 4¼"

Triangles

J
6¾" x 6¾"
Cut two squares. Cut on the diagonal both ways to make 8 triangles.

K
3¾" x 3¾"
Cut two squares. Cut on the diagonal one way to make 4 triangles.

To Assemble:

Blocks:

Refer to general instructions for how to sew pieces together into blocks.

Start with center square E and add log E. Next, add light log F, then dark log F. Continue adding logs G, H, and I, as in Figure 1.

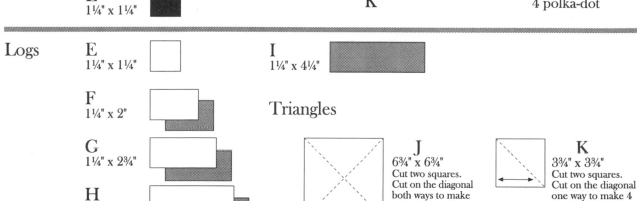

Figure 1

Rows:

Refer to the section in the general instructions called "Sewing the Blocks Together". This explains construction of rows into a finished top. The rows will be constructed as shown in Figure 2.

After all the rows are sewn together, measure for side borders. Cut two side borders and sew them on. Measure for the top and bottom borders and add them.

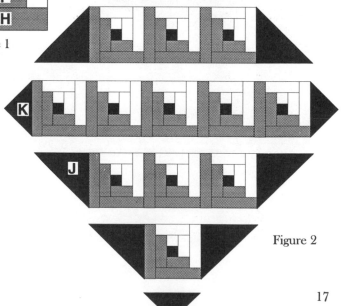

Figure 2

Topsy Turvy Log Cabin

Shown on inside back cover

15½" x 17½"
3¼" blocks - 16 blocks set 4 x 4

Templates needed: T, Z, V, W, X, E

Topsy Turvy Log Cabin

The color scheme in this quilt is basically tan and black with red center squares. The blocks are made with one set of dark logs and two sets of light logs. I flipped the blocks different ways and added a few triangles to this quilt. Red ¼" piping and top and bottom black borders add more interest. Hand quilted.

Cutting Instructions:

For this quilt, the center squares were all cut from the same red fabric. The dark and light logs were cut from a variety of prints. I used red squares added to some of the long light logs to form the triangles.

Following the general directions, cut pieces either using templates and scissors or rotary cutter.

Borders:

Side - cut 2 1½" x length of top
Top & Bottom -
Inner & Outer: cut 1½" x width of top after side borders are added, 2 for inner, 2 for outer.

	Per Block	Total
T	1 center	16 center
Z	1 light	16 light
V	1 light, 1 dark	16 light, 16 dark
W	1 light, 1 dark	16 light, 16 dark
X	1 light	16 light
E		8

Center Square

T
1½" x 1½"

Logs

Z
1¼" x 1½"

V
1¼" x 2¼"

W
1¼" x 3"

X
1¼" x 3¾"

E
1¼" x 1¼"

Blocks:

Prepare half (8) of the logs X before constructing the block. Place square E at one end of the log X, right sides together. Stitch along the diagonal, trim extra and finger-press the seam towards the dark fabric. See Figure 1 for placement and which diagonal to sew.

Refer to the general directions for how to sew the pieces together into blocks. Start with the center square T, add log Z. Add light log V to the right side. Add dark log V to the bottom. Add dark log W to the left side, light log W on top and finish with log X on the right side. Note the orientation of log X with the added triangle (Figure 2).

Rows:

Refer to the section in the general instructions called "Sewing the Blocks Together". This explains construction of rows into a finished top. Following the color photograph and drawing, arrange the blocks in rows.

Borders:

After the blocks are sewn together, measure the length of the top and cut the side borders. Add the side borders. Measure the width and cut the top and bottom borders (inner and outer). Add the inner top and bottom border. Add the outer top and bottom border. If you wish to add piping around the blocks, cut a piece of fabric 1" by a measurement four times the width of the top. Fold in half and insert in the seam as you add the side borders and the inner top and bottom borders.

Cut along this line

Figure 1

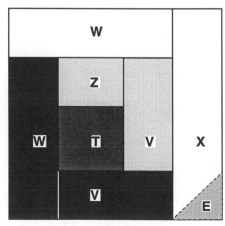

Figure 2

Stretch It Rectangular

Shown on inside back cover

16" x 18"
4" x 4½" blocks, set 4 x 4

Templates needed:
    U, F, V, G, W, H, X, I, Y

Stretch It Rectangular

Beginning with a rectangle in the middle, instead of a square, results in rectangular blocks. Four blocks wide and four blocks long automatically becomes a rectangular quilt.

Cutting Instructions:

The center "squares" (rectangles) were cut from the same red fabric. Dark logs were cut from a variety of dark prints. Different light prints were used for the light side.

Following the general directions, cut pieces either using templates and scissors or rotary cutter.

	Per Block	Total
U	1 center	16 center
F	1 dark	16 dark
V	1 dark	16 dark
G	1 light	16 light
W	1 light	16 light
H	1 dark	16 dark
X	1 dark	16 dark
I	1 light	16 light
Y	1 light	16 light

Center "Square"

U
1½" x 2"

Logs

F
1¼" x 2"

V
1¼" x 2¼"

G
1¼" x 2¾"

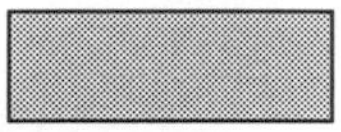

W
1¼" x 3"

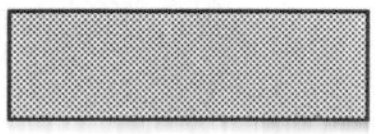

H
1¼" x 3½"

X
1¼" x 3¾"

I
1¼" x 4¼"

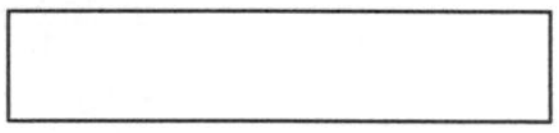

Y
1¼" x 4½"

To Assemble:

Blocks:

Refer to general instructions for how to sew pieces together into blocks.

Start with center "square" U, add dark log F. Continue around adding dark log V, light log G, light log W, dark log H, dark log X, light log I and ending with light log Y.

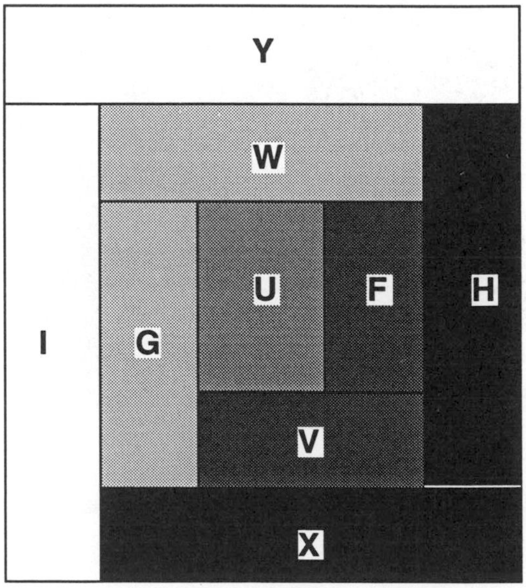

Rows:

Refer to the section in the general instructions called "Sewing the Blocks Together". This explains construction of rows into a finished top. Following the color photograph and drawing, be sure to arrange the blocks so the colors form the straight furrows pattern.

Log Cabin
with Sashing
Shown on inside front cover

17¼" x 20"
3¾" blocks - 12 blocks set 3 x 4 with sashing

Templates needed: E, F, G, H, I, S, T

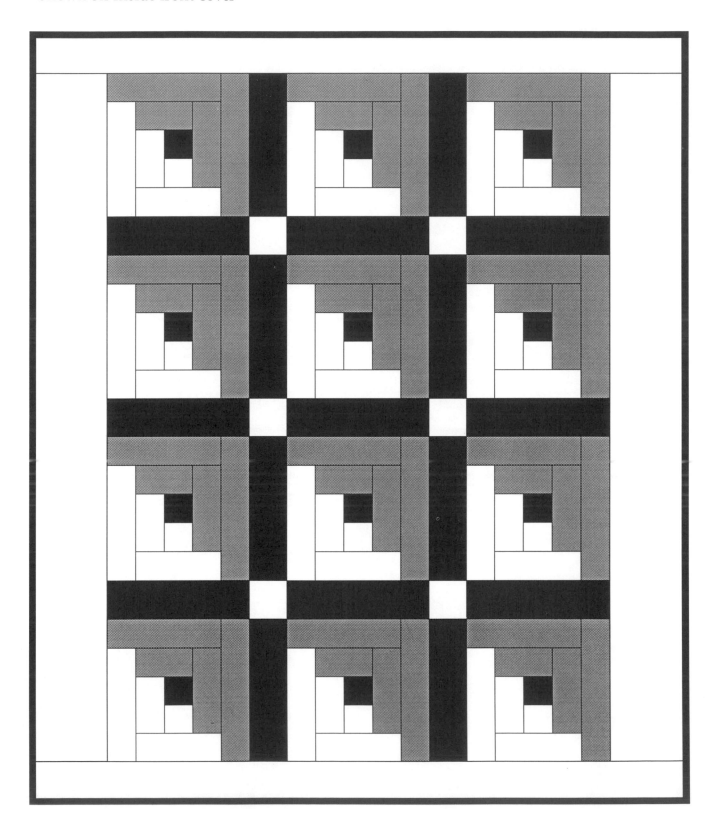

Log Cabin with Sashing

These standard log cabin blocks are all set the same direction and separated by purple sashing. The color scheme is a lavender and yellow, and all the blocks are identical. The purple print in the sashing is repeated in the binding.

Cutting Instructions:

For this quilt, five different fabrics were used. The center squares and sashing rectangles were cut from the same dark fabric. For the "dark" side of the block, two medium prints were used. The "light" side of the block was cut from two prints. One of these was used for the sashing squares, and the other light print was used for the border.

Following the general directions, cut pieces either using templates and scissors or rotary cutter.

	Per Block	Total
E	1 center, 1 light	20 center, 20 light
F	1 light, 1 med	20 light, 20 med
G	1 light, 1 med	20 light, 20 med
H	1 light, 1 med	20 light, 20 med
I	1 med	20 med
S		17 dark
T		6 light

Borders:

Side - Cut 2½" x length of top
Top and Bottom - Cut 1½" x width of top after adding side borders.

Center Square

E
1¼" x 1¼"

Logs

E
1¼" x 1¼"

F
1¼" x 2"

G
1¼" x 2¾"

H
1¼" x 3½"

I
1¼" x 4¼"

Sashing

S
1½" x 4¼"

T
1½" x 1½"

To Assemble:

Blocks:

Refer to general instructions for how to sew pieces together into blocks.

Start with center square E and add log E.
Next, add light log F, then dark log F. Continue adding logs G, H, and I.

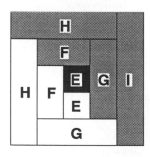

Rows:

Refer to the section in the general instructions called "Sewing the Blocks Together". This explains construction of rows into a finished top.

For this quilt, you will add sashing rectangles S between the blocks. Sashing rows between the block rows are made of rectangles S and squares T. Make three of the sashing rows.

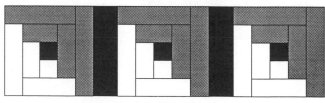

Blocks with sashing

Sashing Row

Red Corner Stones

Shown on inside front cover

15" x 18¾"
3¾" blocks - 20 blocks set 4 x 5

Templates needed: E, F, G, H

Templates - These are for machine piecing and include the
¼" seam allowance.

A
2½" x 2½"

H
1¼" x 3½"

G
1¼" x 2¾"

B
1½" x 2½"

F
1¼" x 2"

C
1½" x 3½"

Z
1¼" x 1½"

Plate 1

Templates - These are for machine piecing and include the ¼" seam allowance.

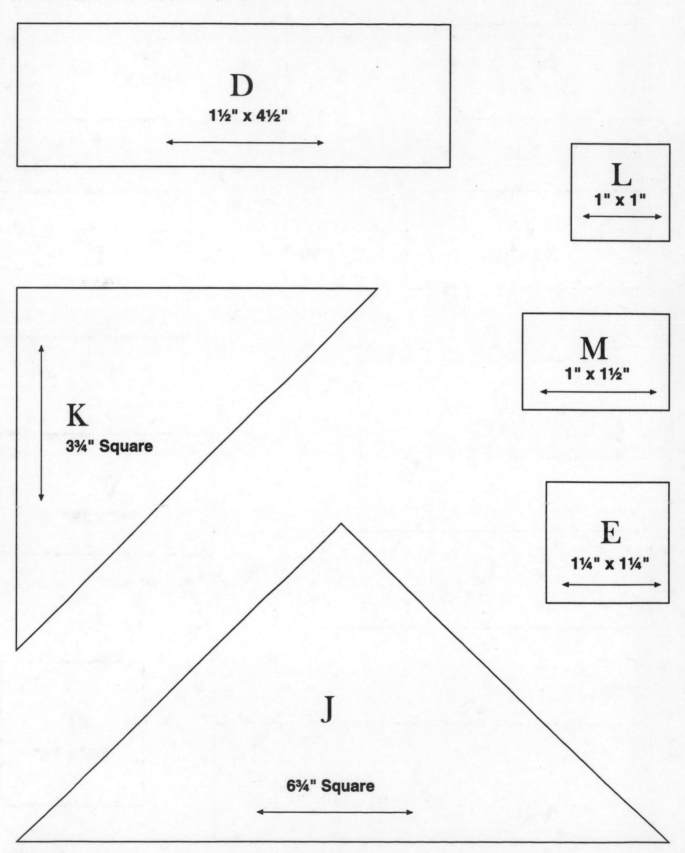

D
1½" x 4½"

L
1" x 1"

M
1" x 1½"

K
3¾" Square

E
1¼" x 1¼"

J
6¾" Square

Plate 2

Templates - These are for machine piecing and include the ¼" seam allowance.

N
1" x 2"

W
1¼" x 3"

O
1" x 2½"

U
1½" x 2"

P
1" x 3"

V
1¼" x 2¼"

Q
1" x 3½"

Y
1¼" x 4½"

T
1½" x 1½"

Plate 3

Templates - These are for machine piecing and include the
¼" seam allowance.

X
1¼" x 3¾"

R
1" x 4"

I
1¼" x 4¼"

S
1½" x 4¼"

AA
1" x 4½"

Plate 4

Red Corner Stones

This variation is created by adding red squares to the end of every dark log. High contrast between the darks and lights creates a more dramatic pattern. When adding the logs, it is easiest to make the red squares line up exactly if you start sewing at the end with the red square. Line it up matching the seams and sew each log in place. This quilt is machine quilted in the ditch and diagonally through the red squares. The diagonal quilting lines help emphasize the set.

Cutting Instructions:

For this quilt, the center squares and stones were all cut from the same red fabric. The dark and light logs were cut from a variety of prints.

Following the general directions, cut pieces either using templates and scissors or rotary cutter.

	Per Block	Total
E	1 light, 1 dark, 5 red	20 light, 20 dark, 100 red
F	1 light, 1 dark	20 light, 20 dark
G	1 light, 1 dark	20 light, 20 dark
H	1 light, 1 dark	20 light, 20 dark

Center Square and Stones

E
1¼" x 1¼"

Logs

E
1¼" x 1¼"

F
1¼" x 2"

G
1¼" x 2¾"

H
1¼" x 3½"

To Assemble:

Blocks:

Prepare logs before constructing blocks. Add a red square E to the end of dark logs E, F, G and H.

Refer to the general directions for how to sew the pieces together into blocks. Start with center square E.
Add logs in the following order:
     light log E to the left side
     light log F to the top
     pieced log (dark E)-(red E) to the right
     pieced log (dark F)-(red E) to the bottom
     light log G to the left
     light log H to the top
     pieced log (dark G)-(red E) to the right
Finish with adding pieced log (dark H)-(red E) to the bottom.

Rows:

Refer to the section in the general instructions called "Sewing the Blocks Together". This explains construction of rows into a finished top. Following the color photograph and drawing, arrange the blocks in rows to achieve the barn raising set.

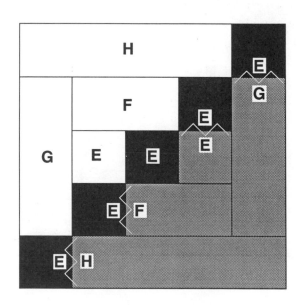

Light and Dark

Shown on inside back cover

14" x 17½"
3½" blocks - 20 blocks set 4 x 5

Templates needed: L, M, N, O,
P, Q, R

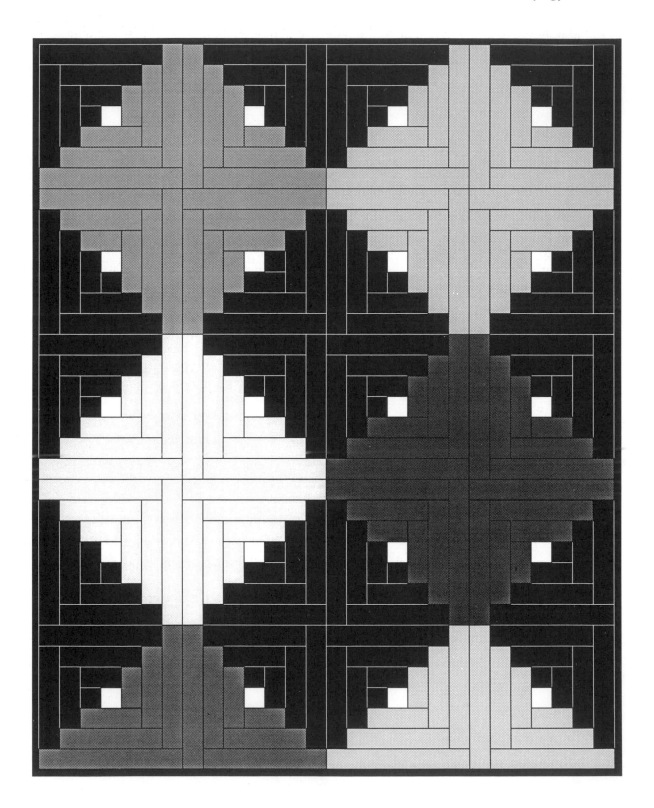

Light and Dark

Groups of four identical blocks are used to create this quilt. The gold center squares look like little lights. The quilt is tied on the back with dark cotton floss.

Cutting Instructions:

For this quilt, the center squares were all cut from the same gold fabric. The "dark" side of the block was cut from black fabric. The "light" side was cut from a variety of solid fabrics, with four groups of four blocks each cut from the same color and two groups of two blocks each cut from the same color.

Following the general directions, cut pieces either using templates and scissors or rotary cutter.

	Per Block	Total
L	1 center, 1 dark	20 center, 20 dark
M	1 light, 1 dark	20 light, (4/set) 20 dark
N	1 light, 1 dark	20 light (4/set), 20 dark
O	1 light, 1 dark	20 light (4/set), 20 dark
P	1 light, 1 dark	20 light (4/set), 20 dark
Q	1 light, 1 dark	20 light (4/set), 20 dark
R	1 light	20 light (4/set)

Center Square

L
1" x 1"

Logs

L
1" x 1"

M
1" x 1½"

N
1" x 2"

O
1" x 2½"

P
1" x 3"

Q
1" x 3½"

R
1" x 4"

To Assemble:

Blocks:

Refer to general instructions for how to sew pieces together into blocks.

Start with center square L and add dark log L. Next, add dark log M, then light log M. Continue adding light and dark logs N, O, P, Q and R.

Rows:

Refer to the section in the general instructions called "Sewing the Blocks Together". This explains construction of rows into a finished top. Following the color photograph and drawing, be sure to arrange the blocks in rows so the colors form the light and dark pattern.

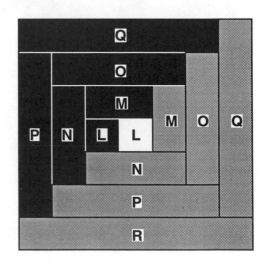

Blue Zig Zag

Shown on inside back cover

14" x 17½"
3½" blocks - 20 blocks set 4 x 5

Templates needed: L, M, N, O,
P, Q, R

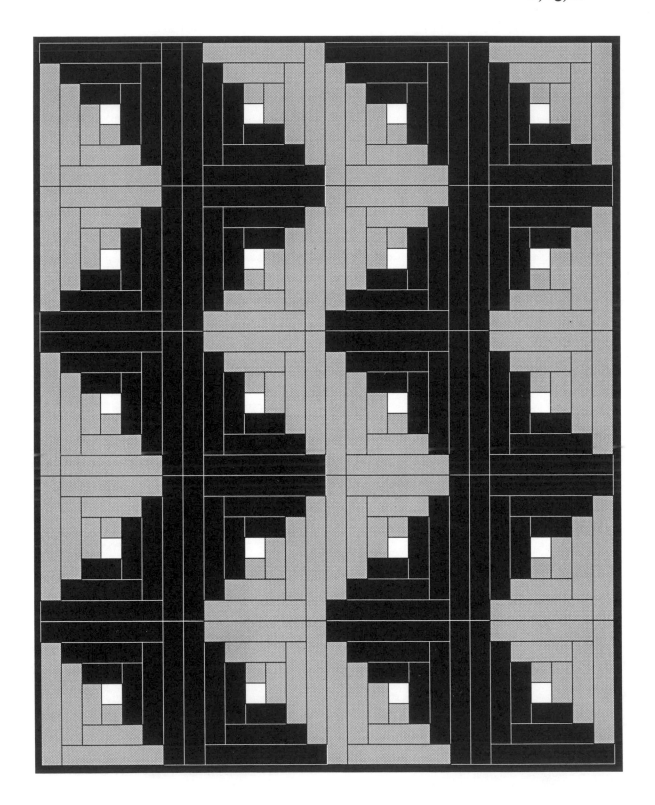

Blue Zig Zag

The Zig Zag set is strongest when made with logs of just two highly contrasting colors. The blue is solid and the black is a print with blue and green lines. This quilt is tied on the back with black thread.

Cutting Instructions:

The centers of all the blocks were cut from the same red fabric. The light logs were cut from the same blue solid, and the same black print was used for all the dark logs.

Following the general directions, cut pieces either using templates and scissors or rotary cutter.

	Per Block	Total
L	1 center, 1 light	20 center, 20 light
M	1 light, 1 dark	20 light, 20 dark
N	1 light, 1 dark	20 light, 20 dark
O	1 light, 1 dark	20 light, 20 dark
P	1 light, 1 dark	20 light, 20 dark
Q	1 light, 1 dark	20 light, 20 dark
R	1 dark	20 dark

Center Square

L
1" x 1"

Logs

L
1" x 1"

M
1" x 1½"

N
1" x 2"

O
1" x 2½"

P
1" x 3"

Q
1" x 3½"

R
1" x 4"

To Assemble:

Blocks:

Refer to general instructions for how to sew pieces together into blocks.

Start with center square L and add light log L.
Next, add light log M, then dark log M. Continue adding light and dark logs N, O, P, Q and R.

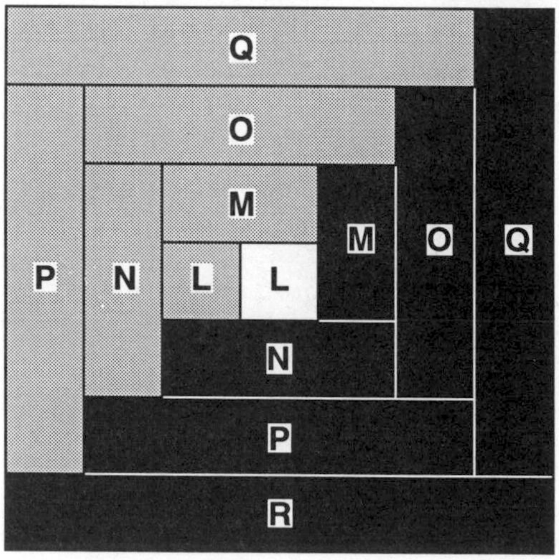

Rows:

Refer to the section in the general instructions called "Sewing the Blocks Together". This explains construction of rows into a finished top. Following the color photograph and drawing, be sure to arrange the blocks in rows so the colors form the zig zag pattern.

Scrappy Light and Dark

Shown on inside back cover

14" x 17½"
3½" blocks - 20 blocks set 4 x 5

Templates needed: L, M, N, O, P, Q, R

Scrappy Light and Dark

This quilt is made with a wide variety of solid colors. The high contrast between the light and dark fabrics helps the over-all pattern to show clearly. The quilt is tied at the junctions of all the blocks with gold embroidery floss on the back of the quilt.

Cutting Instructions:

The centers of all the blocks were cut from the same red fabric. A variety of dark and light solids was used for the logs.

Following the general directions, cut pieces either using templates and scissors or rotary cutter.

	Per Block	Total
L	1 center, 1 dark	20 center, 20 dark
M	1 light, 1 dark	20 light, 20 dark
N	1 light, 1 dark	20 light, 20 dark
O	1 light, 1 dark	20 light, 20 dark
P	1 light, 1 dark	20 light, 20 dark
Q	1 light, 1 dark	20 light, 20 dark
R	1 light	20 light

Center Square

L
1" x 1"

Logs

L
1" x 1"

M
1" x 1½"

N
1" x 2"

O
1" x 2½"

P
1" x 3"

Q
1" x 3½"

R
1" x 4"

To Assemble:

Blocks:

Refer to general instructions for how to sew pieces together into blocks.

Start with center square L and add dark log L. Next, add dark log M, then light log M. Continue adding light and dark logs N, O, P, Q and R.

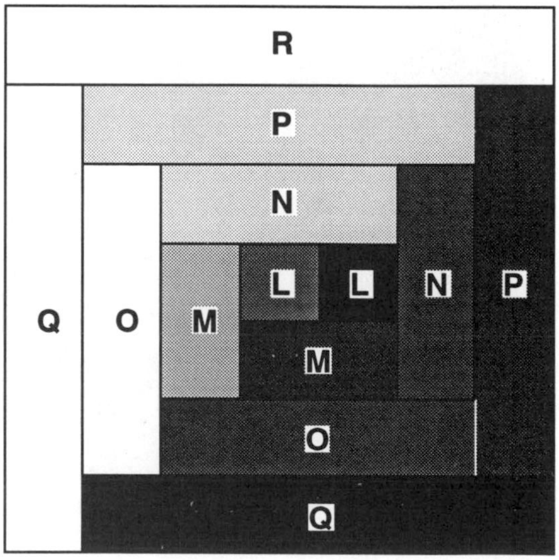

Rows:

Refer to the section in the general instructions called "Sewing the Blocks Together". This explains construction of rows into a finished top. Following the color photograph and drawing, be sure to arrange the blocks in rows so the colors form the light and dark pattern.

Pinwheel Log Cabin

Shown on inside front cover

16½" x 18"
3½" blocks - 16 blocks set 4 x 4

Templates needed: L, M, N, O,
P, Q, R

Pinwheel Log Cabin

Three slightly different tones of solid gold are combined with four different plaids and a dark solid in this quilt. The blocks are set to form pinwheels. The center of the quilt is tied in gold pearl cotton, and the border is tied in dark purple.

Cutting Instructions:

The center squares were cut from the same fabric. The blocks are in groups of four to form the pinwheel. Four different dark fabrics are used, one per group of four.

Following the general directions, cut pieces either using templates and scissors or rotary cutter.

Borders:

Side borders - Cut 1¾" x length of top
Top & bottom - Cut 2½" x width of top, after side borders are added.

	Per Block	Total
L	1 center, 1 dark	16 center, 16 dark
M	1 light, 1 dark	16 light, 16 dark (4/set)
N	1 light, 1 dark	16 light, 16 dark (4/set)
O	1 light, 1 dark	16 light, 16 dark (4/set)
P	1 light, 1 dark	16 light, 16 dark (4/set)
Q	1 light, 1 dark	16 light, 16 dark (4/set)
R	1 light	16 light

Center Square

L
1" x 1"

Logs

L
1" x 1"

M
1" x 1½"

N
1" x 2"

O
1" x 2½"

P
1" x 3"

Q
1" x 3½"
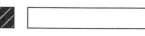

R
1" x 4"

To Assemble:

Blocks:

Refer to general instructions for how to sew pieces together into blocks.

Start with center square L and add dark log L. Next, add dark log M, then light log M. Continue adding light and dark logs N, O, P, Q and R.

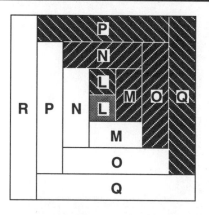

Rows:

Refer to the section in the general instructions called "Sewing the Blocks Together". This explains construction of rows into a finished top. Following the color photograph and drawing, be sure to arrange the blocks in rows so the colors form the pinwheel pattern.

After blocks are sewn together, measure and cut side borders. Sew borders on. Measure width and cut top and bottom borders. Sew these borders on.

Set Combination

Shown on inside front cover

15" x 18¾"
3¾" blocks - 20 blocks set 4 x 5

Templates needed: E, F, G, H, I

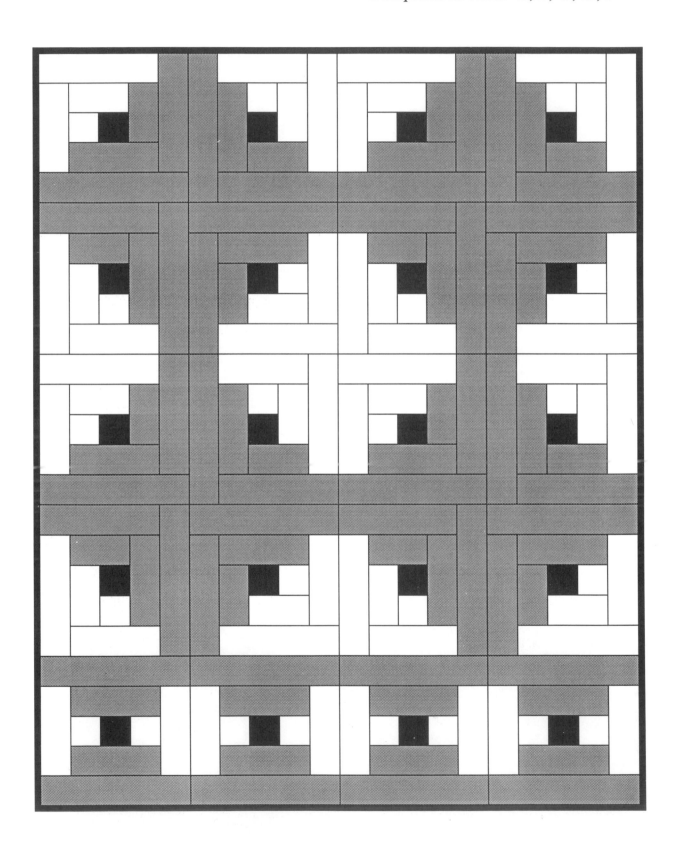

Set Combination

Red centers and two prints make up this quilt. The green is what I think of as a busy print. It has a lot going on and strong contrast in the colors. The red center squares seem to pop out, since red and green next to each other vibrate. This quilt combines two log cabin sets. Most of the quilt is done in the Light and Dark set with one row of Court House Step blocks. Hand quilted.

Cutting Instructions:

For this quilt, the center squares were all cut from the same red fabric. All the dark logs were cut from one print as were the light logs.

Following the general directions, cut pieces either using templates and scissors or rotary cutter.

Center Square

E
1¼" x 1¼"

	Log Cabin Block	Court House Block	Total
E	1 center, 1 light	1 center, 2 light	20 center, 24 light
F	1 light, 1 dark		16 light, 16 dark
G	1 light, 1 dark	2 light, 2 dark	24 light, 24 dark
H	1 light, 1 dark		16 light, 16 dark
I	1 dark	2 dark	24 dark

Logs

E
1¼" x 1¼"

F
1¼" x 2"

G
1¼" x 2¾"

H
1¼" x 3½"

I
1¼" x 4¼"

To Assemble:

Blocks:

Sixteen blocks are made in the regular log cabin manner and can be made as described in the general directions. Start with center square E, add light log E to the bottom. Add light log F to the right. Continue to add logs around - dark F, dark G, light G, light H, dark H and end with dark I.

Four of the blocks are constructed in the Court House Steps method. Start with center square E, add light log E to both sides. Dark G logs are added to the top and bottom, then light log G is added to the sides. End with dark log I added to the top and bottom.

Rows:

Refer to the section in the general instructions called "Sewing the Blocks Together". This explains construction of rows into a finished top. Arrange the blocks so the log cabin blocks are in the light and dark configuration. The last row is made of the four court house steps blocks.

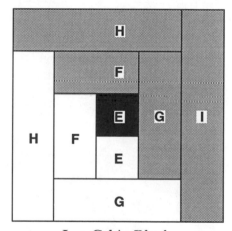

Log Cabin Block

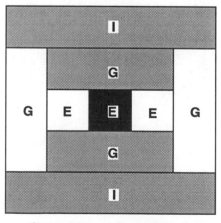

Court House Steps Block

35

In the Pink

Shown on inside front cover

14½" x 18"
2½" blocks - 30 blocks set 5 x 6

Templates needed: L, N, P

In the Pink

A new pattern is created when you place blocks next to each other that contain the same color or print. This quilt is tied in lavender pearl cotton at the centers and corners of every block.

Borders:

Side borders - Cut 2 pieces 1½" x length of top
Top & bottom - Measure width after adding side borders, cut 2 pieces 2" x width.

Center Square

L
1" x 1"

Logs

L
1" x 1"

N
1" x 2"

P
1" x 3"

Cutting Instructions:

For this quilt, the center squares were all cut from the same red fabric. The dark and light logs could be cut from the same fabrics, or use some variety as seen in the photo.

Following the general directions, cut pieces either using templates and scissors or rotary cutter.

	Per Block	Total
L	1 center, 2 light	30 center, 60 light
N	2 light, 2 dark	60 light, 60 dark
P	2 dark	60 dark

To Assemble:

Blocks:

This block is constructed in the Court House Steps method. Instead of going around the center square, the logs are added to the sides, then to the top and bottom. Refer to the general directions for how to chain piece.

Start with center square L and add a light log L to the top and bottom. Add dark log N to both sides. Add light log N to top and bottom. Finish with adding dark log P to both sides.

Rows:

Refer to the section in the general instructions called "Sewing the Blocks Together". This explains construction of rows into a finished top. Following the color photograph and drawing, arrange the blocks in rows.

Borders:

After the blocks are sewn together, measure the length and cut the side borders. Add side borders. Measure width and cut top and bottom borders. Finish by adding the top and bottom borders.

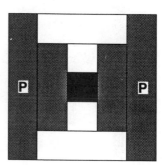

Japanese Lanterns

Shown on inside back cover

14" x 17½"
3½" blocks - 20 blocks set 4 x 5

Templates needed: L, N, P, R

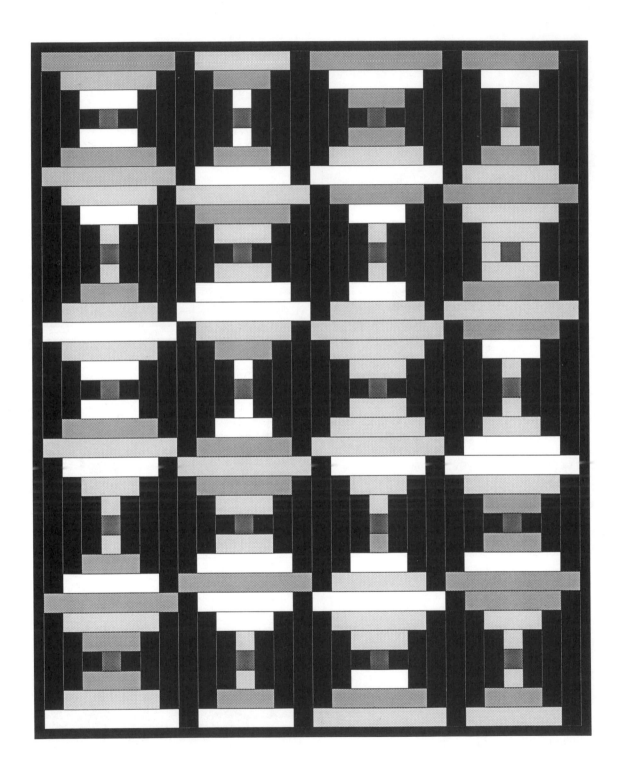

Japanese Lanterns

I named this quilt in honor of the quilting friends I made on my visit to Japan. The blocks in this quilt are the same except every other block is made with a light and dark reversal; then the block is rotated. The dark green is consistent throughout the quilt, while the lights include five tones in tans and grays.

Cutting Instructions:

For this quilt, the center squares were all cut from the same red fabric. The dark logs were all cut from the same dark green fabric. The light logs were cut from five different tans and grays.

Following the general directions, cut pieces either using templates and scissors or rotary cutter.

	Light Block	Dark Block	Total
L	1 center, 2 dark	1 center, 2 light	20 cntr, 20 lt, 20 drk
N	2 light, 2 dark	2 light, 2 dark	40 light, 40 dark
P	2 light, 2 dark	2 light, 2 dark	40 light, 40 dark
R	2 light	2 dark	20 light, 20 dark

Center Square
L
1" x 1"

Logs

L
1" x 1"

N
1" x 2"

P
1" x 3"

R
1" x 4"

To Assemble:

Blocks:

This block is constructed in the Court House Steps method. Instead of going around the center square, the logs are added to the sides, then to the top and bottom. Refer to the General Directions for tips on chain piecing.

For a "Dark" block, start with center square L and add a light log L to the top and bottom. Add dark log N to the sides. Continue adding logs to the top and bottom (light N), then sides (dark P) as shown in the figure. For the last "round", add light log P to the top and bottom, then add dark log R to the sides for the last logs.

The "Light" block is made in a similar way. Follow the block drawing for order of adding the logs.

Rows:

Refer to the section in the general instructions called "Sewing the Blocks Together". This explains construction of rows into a finished top. Following the color photograph and drawing, arrange the blocks in rows.

"Dark" Block

"Light" Block

Ring Around the Rosy

Shown on inside back cover

14" x 17½"
3½" blocks - 20 blocks set 4 x 5

Templates needed: L, N, P, R

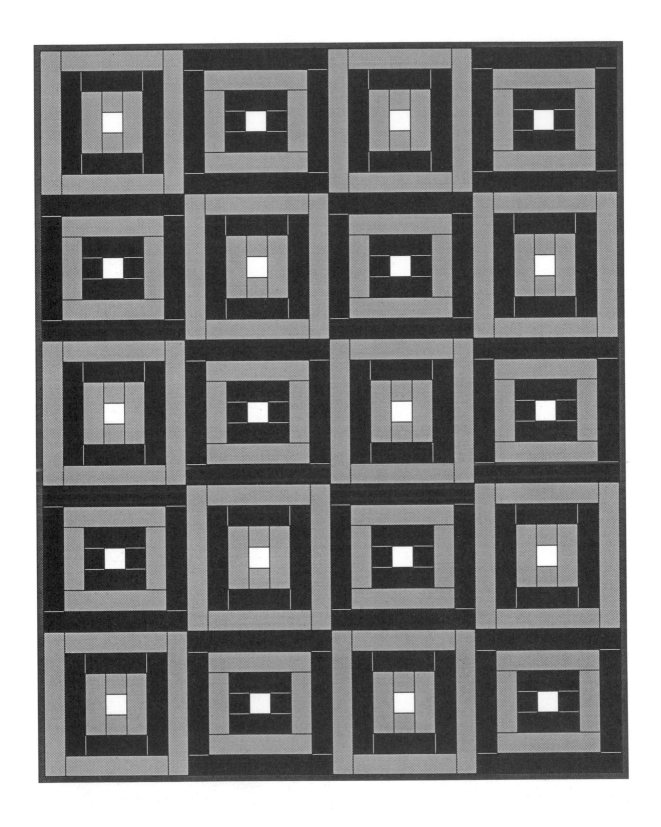

Ring Around the Rosy

In this quilt, the colors go all the way around the block, instead of being diagonally divided between lights and darks. Basically, two different blocks alternate to make this quilt. Five of the blocks incorporate a peach color as a replacement for the tan color. This quilt has an orderly look about it, interrupted only by the asymmetrical placement of the blocks containing the substitute peach color.

Cutting Instructions:

For this quilt, the center squares were all cut from the same red fabric. The dark and light logs could be cut from the same fabrics, or use some variety as seen in the photo.

Following the general directions, cut pieces either using templates and scissors or rotary cutter.

		Light Block	Dark Block	Total
	L	1 center, 2 light	1 center, 2 dark	20 cntr, 20 lt, 20 drk
	N	2 light, 2 dark	2 light, 2 dark	40 light, 40 dark
Center Square	P	2 light, 2 dark	2 light, 2 dark	40 light, 40 dark
L	R	2 light	2 dark	20 light, 20 dark
1" x 1"				

Logs

L 1" x 1"

N 1" x 2"

P 1" x 3"

R 1" x 4"

To Assemble:

Blocks:

This block is constructed in the Court House Steps method. Instead of going around the center square, the logs are added to the sides, then to the top and bottom.

For a "Dark" block, start with center square L and add a dark log L to both sides. Add dark log N to the top and bottom. Continue adding logs to the sides (light N), then top and bottom (light P) as shown in the figure. For the last "round", add dark P to the sides, then add dark R to the top and bottom.

The "Light" block is made in a similar way. Follow the block drawing for order of adding logs.

Rows:

Refer to the section in the general instructions called "Sewing the Blocks Together". This explains construction of rows into a finished top. Following the color photograph and drawing, arrange the blocks in rows so the dark and light blocks alternate.

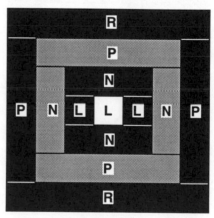

"Dark" Block

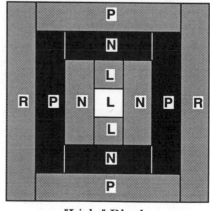

"Light" Block

Small Beginnings

Shown on inside back cover

14½" x 18"
4" blocks - 12 blocks set 3 x 4

Templates needed: M, O, Q, T, AA

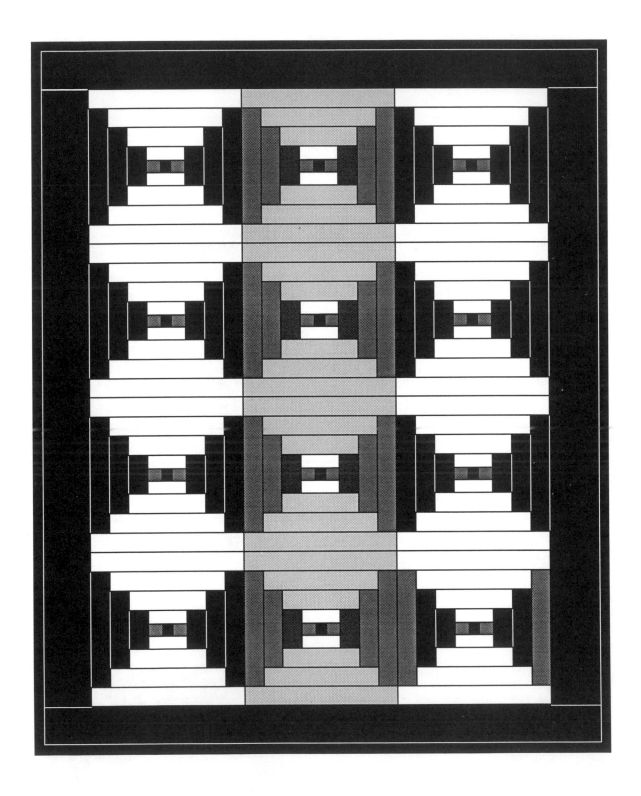

Small Beginnings

This is a standard Court House Steps block, except it begins with little ¼" court house steps as a middle composition. The rest of the quilt is ½" finished logs, half light and half dark, in a variety of solid colors.

Cutting Instructions:

For this quilt, the dark and light logs were cut from a variety of solids. The center square was constructed by strip piecing. Cutting directions are given below.

Following the general directions, cut pieces either using templates and scissors or rotary cutter.

Borders:

Side borders - Cut 2 pieces 1¾" x length of top
Top and bottom borders - Measure width after adding side borders. Cut 2 pieces 1½" x width.

	Per Block	Total
T	1 center	12 center
M	2 dark	24 dark
O	2 light, 2 dark	24 light, 24 dark
Q	2 light, 2 dark	24 light, 24 dark
AA	2 light	24 light

Center Square

T
1½" x 1½"

Logs

M
1" x 1½"

O
1" x 2½"

Q
1" x 3½"

AA
1" x 4½"

The center square will be strip pieced. Cut a strip ¾" x 12". This will be the little center square and was cut from red fabric. Cut 2 strips 1" x 12". Sew these three strips together (Figure 1). Press seams to outside. Cut this strip into ¾" rectangles, 12 total (Figure 2). For the top and bottom row, cut 1" strips. Cut these into 2" rectangles (24 total). Add a rectangle to the top and bottom of the center pieced row. It's OK if the pieces are not exactly the same size. Use template square T to trim to the exact size (Figure 3).

Blocks:

Refer to the general directions for tips on chain piecing. Start with the little pieced center square T. Add dark log M to both sides. Add light log O to the top and bottom. Continue adding to sides, then top and bottom, following the block drawing (Figure 4).

Rows:

Refer to the section in the general instructions called "Sewing the Blocks Together". This explains construction of rows into a finished top. Following the color photograph and drawing, arrange the blocks in rows.

Borders:

After the blocks are sewn together, measure the length and cut the side borders. Add side borders. Measure width and cut top and bottom borders. Finish by sewing the top and bottom borders.

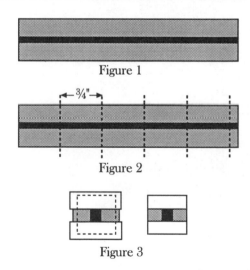

Figure 1

¾"

Figure 2

Figure 3

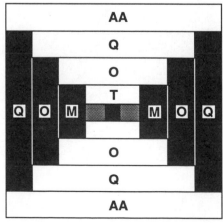

Figure 4

Interlocking Steps

Shown on back cover

14" x 17½"
3½" blocks - 20 blocks set 4 x 5

Templates needed: L, N, P, R

Interlocking Steps

In this Court House Steps, the colors in each block correspond with the colors of the adjacent blocks on all sides. The pattern is created where the blocks join together.

Cutting Instructions:

For this quilt, the center squares were all cut from the same red fabric. The dark logs were all cut from the same black fabric. To achieve the look of this quilt, careful planning is required for cutting the light logs. Half the light logs from one block are the same fabric as half the light logs in the adjacent block.

Following the general directions, cut pieces either using templates and scissors or rotary cutter.

	Per Block	Total
L	1 center, 2 dark	20 center, 40 dark
N	2 light, 2 dark	40 light, 40 dark
P	2 light, 2 dark	40 light, 40 dark
R	2 light	40 light

Center Square

L
1" x 1"

Logs

L
1" x 1"

N
1" x 2"

P
1" x 3"

R
1" x 4"

To Assemble:

Blocks:

This block is constructed in the Court House Steps method. Instead of going around the center square, the logs are added to the sides, then to the top and bottom. Refer to the general directions for tips on chain piecing.

Begin with center square L and add dark log L to both sides. Add light log N to the top and bottom. Continue adding logs to the sides, then top and bottom, following the block diagram.

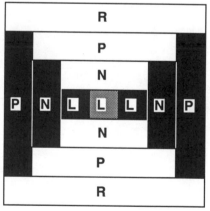

Block

Rows:

Refer to the section in the general instructions called "Sewing the Blocks Together". This explains construction of rows into a finished top. Following the color photograph and drawing, arrange the blocks in rows, matching the tops and bottoms of the blocks with the same colors.

Crazy Log Cabin

14" x 17½"
3½" blocks - 20 blocks set 4 x 5

Shown on back cover

Crazy Log Cabin

What to do with all the leftover scraps from the first nineteen Log Cabin Quilts? Sew them together into a crazy Log Cabin! This free-wheeling little quilt was made by sewing the logs together in any way that occurred to me. It includes some experimental blocks and some left-over blocks from other quilts in this book. Most of the blocks were made with ½" finished logs.

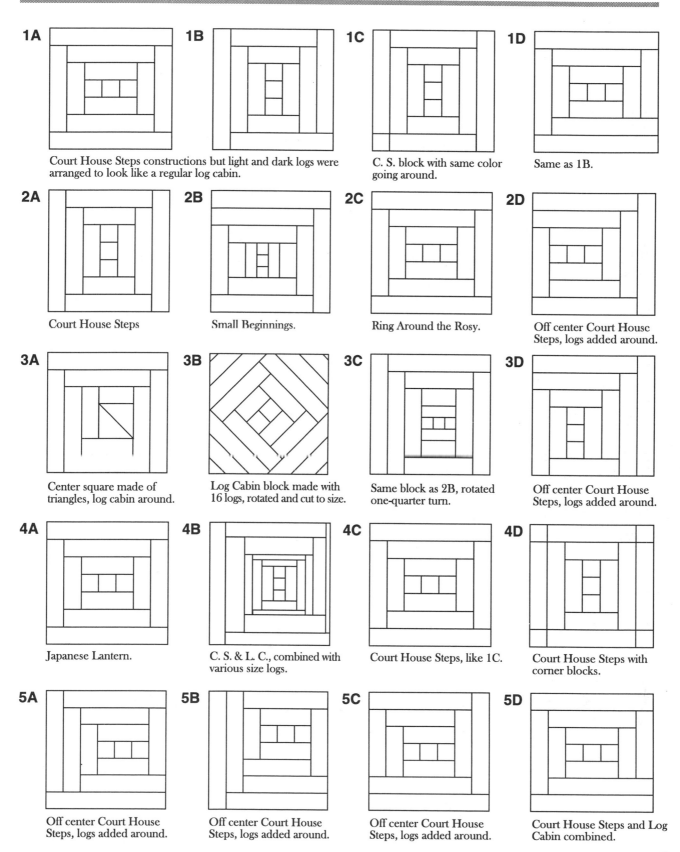

1A Court House Steps constructions but light and dark logs were arranged to look like a regular log cabin.

1B

1C C. S. block with same color going around.

1D Same as 1B.

2A Court House Steps

2B Small Beginnings.

2C Ring Around the Rosy.

2D Off center Court House Steps, logs added around.

3A Center square made of triangles, log cabin around.

3B Log Cabin block made with 16 logs, rotated and cut to size.

3C Same block as 2B, rotated one-quarter turn.

3D Off center Court House Steps, logs added around.

4A Japanese Lantern.

4B C. S. & L. C., combined with various size logs.

4C Court House Steps, like 1C.

4D Court House Steps with corner blocks.

5A Off center Court House Steps, logs added around.

5B Off center Court House Steps, logs added around.

5C Off center Court House Steps, logs added around.

5D Court House Steps and Log Cabin combined.